MATCH!

JOKE BOOK!

MACMILLAN CHILDREN'S BOOKS

MY FACTFILE!

FILL IN YOUR FOOTY DETAILS!

MY NAME IS...

MY FAVOURITE FOOTBALL TEAM IS...

MY FAVOURITE PLAYER IS...

THE POSITION I PLAY IN IS...

THE TEAMS I PLAY FOR ARE...

MY FAVOURITE FOOTBALL BOOTS ARE...

First published 2019 by Macmillan Children's Books
an imprint of Pan Macmillan
The Smithson, 6 Briset Street, London EC1M 5NR
Associated companies throughout the world
www.panmacmillan.com

ISBN 978-1-5290-2667-2

Pan Macmillan does not have any control over, or any responsibility for,
any author or third-party websites referred to in or on this book.

1 3 5 7 9 8 6 4 2

A CIP catalogue record for this book is available from
the British Library.

Compiled and illustrated by Perfect Bound Ltd
Illustrated by Dan Newman

Printed and bound by GGP Media GmbH, Poessneck

Contents

Kick off

Why are mummies rubbish at football?

They're too wrapped up in themselves.

What do you do when a football is in the air?

Use your head!

Why was the pitch in such a bad mood?

It was fed up of being treated like dirt.

What can light up a dull evening?

A football match.

When is a footballer like a baby?
When they dribble.

How do you stop a hot and sweaty footballer from smelling?
Put a peg on his nose!

How can a footballer stop their nose running?

Tackle it and trip it up.

What does a football do when it rolls to a halt?
Looks round.

What's the difference between Prince Charles and a throw-in?

One's heir to the throne, the other's thrown into the air.

When is a footballer like a grandfather clock?

When they're a striker.

What position did
Cinderella play?

Sweeper.

And why was she thrown out
of the team?

**Because she kept running
away from the ball.**

Why do ghosts play football?
For the ghouls, of course.

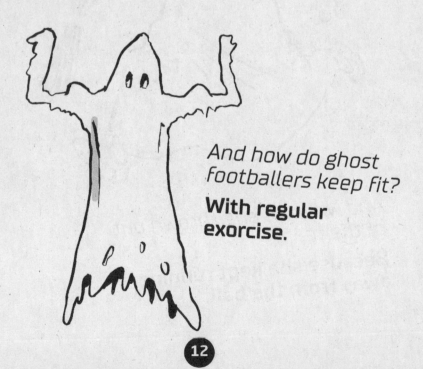

And how do ghost footballers keep fit?
With regular exorcise.

What's the difference between a gutter and a poor keeper?

One catches drops, the other drops catches.

Why did the manager flood the pitch?

He wanted to bring on a sub.

What can a footballer never make right?
Their left foot.

HNNN...

Which goalkeeper can jump higher than the crossbar?
All of them – crossbars can't jump.

How do footballers get their mail?

Through the goal-post service.

The inventor of the red card recently died and the funeral's next week.

He'll get a good send-off.

What do you call an Englishman in the semi-final of the World Cup?

The referee.

Which part of a football pitch smells the nicest?

The scent-er spot.

Why was the ruler no good at football?

He just couldn't measure up.

How can a footballer make more money?

If they fold up a note they'll find it in creases.

Why did the football stop playing the game?

It was tired of being kicked around.

Why did the team get into trouble on the flight out to the World Cup?

They kept running up the wing.

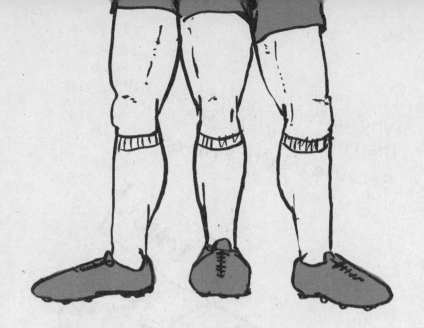

Have you heard about the footballer with three legs?

He's always one step ahead.

Which ghost plays keeper?

The ghoulie, of course!

Why do Velcro boots cost more than boots with laces?

Because they're a rip-off.

What runs all the way round a football pitch but never moves?

A fence.

The toilet facilities at most stadiums are very ordinary.

They're bog standard.

'ARE THERE ANY HOLES IN YOUR FOOTBALL SHORTS?'

'NO, OF COURSE NOT.'

'THEN HOW DO YOU GET THEM ON?'

Footy Favourites

Why did the footballer bring a ball of string on to the pitch?

He was hoping for a tie.

What's the best place to buy a football shirt when you're in America?

New Jersey.

Why was the goalkeeper feeling poorly?

Because he'd forgotten to take his gloves off.

What length are a footballer's shorts?

They must always be above two feet.

Why do footballers always put their right boot on first?

Well, it would be silly to put the wrong boot on, wouldn't it?

What runs around all day and lies still at night with its tongue hanging out?

A football boot.

Why was the snowman no good at football matches?
He kept getting cold feet.

Why did the player throw a bucket of water on the pitch before making his debut?

He wanted to make a big splash.

If it takes 20 players half an hour to eat a ham, how long will it take 40 players to eat half a ham?

That depends on whether they are professionals or am-a-chewers.

I'VE BEEN INVITED TO JOIN MY FIRM'S FOOTBALL TEAM. THEY WANT ME TO PLAY FOR THEM VERY BADLY.

IN THAT CASE, YOU'RE IDEAL FOR IT.

The team kept losing, but the striker shrugged off their run of bad luck. **'After all, what's defeat?'**

'What you're supposed to kick the ball with,' said the manager.

Why did the team sit on the roof at their celebration dinner?
The waiter had told them that the meal was on the house.

A manager gathered his team after a dismal start to the season.

'Right, lads, we need to get back to basics. What I'm holding in my hands is a football, and the object of the game—'

'Whoa, slow down, boss,' called one player. 'You're going too fast.'

THAT NEW PLAYER IS AN ABSOLUTE WONDER.

WHY DO YOU SAY THAT?

BECAUSE I LOOK AT HIM AND WONDER IF HE'S EVER PLAYED BEFORE!

A thief broke into the football club, stole all the entrance money, showered and then left.

He wanted to make a clean getaway.

What do you do if you're too hot at a football match?

Sit next to the fans.

What are the noisiest fans called?

Foot-bawlers.

Footy-mad Animals

Why was the centipede useless at football?

He never got on to the pitch until half-time – it took him so long to lace up his boots!

What position did the ducks play?

Right quack and left quack.

Which footballer can jump the highest?

Wayne Kanga-Rooney.

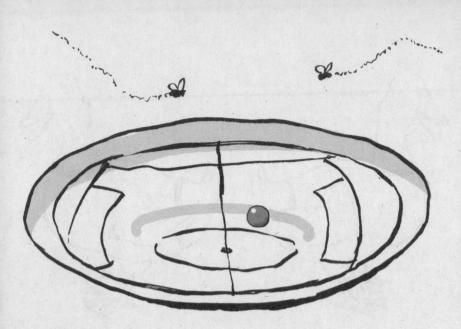

Two flies were playing
football in a saucer.

One said to the other,
**'We'll have to do better
than this; we're playing in
the cup next week!'**

What happened when
the cows played in a
football match?

There was udder chaos.

Why did the chicken
run on to the pitch?

**Because the referee
blew for a fowl.**

Why can't horses play
football?

**Because they've got
two left feet.**

What's large, grey and carries a trunk and two pairs of football boots?

An elephant who's just joined the team.

Why didn't the dog like football?

Because she was a boxer.

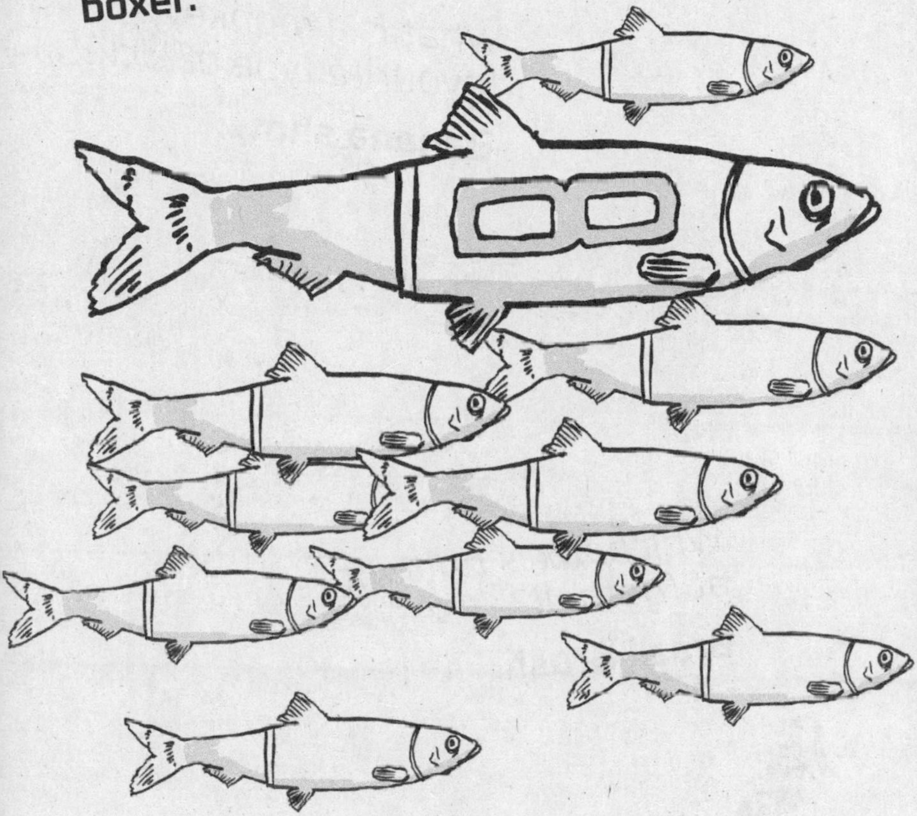

Who is the captain of the fish's football team?

The team's kipper.

What is a monkey's
favourite type of kick?

Banana shots.

Which fox is brilliant
at football?

Brazil Brush.

What did the spider get for Christmas?

Four pairs of football boots.

Which feline is in charge of treating injured players?

The first-aid kit.

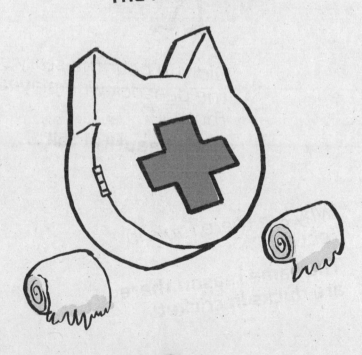

Did you hear the story of the peacock who played football?

It's a beautiful tail . . .

Why are there fouls in football?

The same reason there are ducks in cricket!

Which animal plays football standing on its head?

Yoga Bear.

What's the difference between a flea-ridden dog and a bored football spectator?

One's going to itch; the other's itching to go.

Someone Call for a Doctor!

What happened to the striker after someone threw a pillow at him?

He had a mild concushion.

I'VE GOT A TERRIBLE PAIN IN MY RIGHT FOOT. WHAT SHOULD I DO?

KICK THE BALL WITH YOUR LEFT.

Jordan Henderson tripped over a bottle of Omega-3 capsules during training.

Luckily his injuries are only super-fish-oil.

Doctor: *How's your broken rib?*

Player: *I keep getting a stitch in my side.*

Doctor: *That's good; it shows the bones are knitting.*

A player was hit on the head by a set of tiny bongo drums.

He got a mild percussion.

DOCTOR, DOCTOR. I FEEL LIKE A REFEREE.

DON'T BE SILLY, YOU MUST HAVE SOME FRIENDS.

Player 1: How did you break your leg?

Player 2: See those steps down to the car park?

Player 1: Yes.

Player 2: I didn't.

Doctor, doctor, come quickly! The referee has swallowed his biro! What can we do?

Use a pencil until I get there.

The doctor was giving members of the team a medical.

'Breathe out three times,' he said to one of the players.

'Are you checking my lungs?' asked the player.

'No, I'm cleaning my spectacles,' replied the doctor.

The winger got stretchered off, saying his leg was agony.

When the doctor put his stethoscope on the knee, he heard a tiny voice saying, **'Lend us a tenner, lend us a tenner.'**

'My ankle hurts too,' said the winger, so the doctor listened there as well.

Again there was a little voice, saying, **'Lend us a tenner, lend us a tenner.'**

'I know what's wrong,' said the doctor. **'Your leg's broke in two places.'**

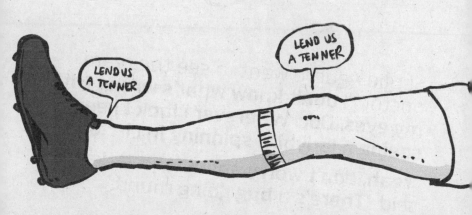

Player: I'm a bit worried my eyesight's not what it was, Doc.

Doctor: You might be right. This is a canteen.

Sergio Aguero went to see the team doctor. 'I don't know what's wrong with my eyes, Doc. Wherever I look I keep seeing a ladybird spinning in circles.'

'Yeah, don't worry about it,' the doctor said. 'There's a bug going round.'

What happened when the footballer went to see his doctor to complain about flat feet?

The doctor gave him a bicycle pump.

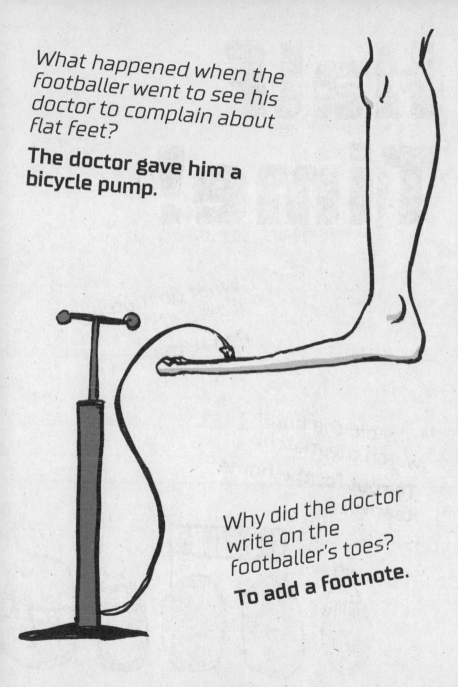

Why did the doctor write on the footballer's toes?

To add a footnote.

Half Time!

What do footballers like to drink?

Penal-tea.

Why did the potato watch the match?

To root for the home team.

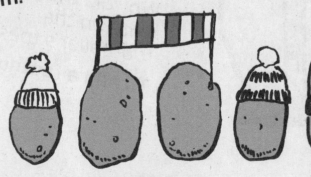

Who was England's best tasting player?

Wayne Macarooney.

What's the difference between the England team and a teabag?

The teabag stays in the cup longer.

Boy: *My mum says she'll leave my dad if he doesn't stop watching football.*

Friend: *Oh dear. That would be awful!*

Boy: *Yes . . . Dad says he'll really miss her!*

What do you call a press photographer taking pictures of the match?

A Flash guy.

Two kids were walking past a house surrounded by a high wall when the owner came out holding a football.

'**Is this your ball?**' he demanded.

'**Er, has it done any damage?**' asked the boy.

'**No,**' said the householder.

'**Then it's ours,**' said the girl.

Why did the man become a marathon runner instead of a footballer?

The doctor told him he had athlete's foot.

What's the best day for a footballer to have a full English for breakfast?

Fry-day.

Why did the footballer put his bed in the fireplace?

He wanted to sleep like a log.

Boss: I thought you wanted the afternoon off to see your dentist.

Woman: That's right.

Boss: Then how come I saw you leaving the football ground with a friend?

Woman: That was my dentist.

Mum: Was there a fight at the match again? You've lost your front teeth!

Boy: No I haven't – they're in my pocket.

Two fleas were leaving a football match when it started to rain.

'Shall we walk?' asked the first flea.

'No,' said the second, **'let's take a dog'**.

What was wrong with the footballer whose nose ran and feet smelt?

He was built upside down.

Why were the girls playing football in the trees?

Because the sign said no ball games on the grass.

Old Butterfingers had let five goals through in the first half. **'Can you spare me 10p?'** he asked the captain. **'I want to call a friend.'**

'Here's 20p,' said the captain. **'Phone all your friends'.**

I'M SORRY I MISSED THE GOAL. I COULD KICK MYSELF!

DON'T BOTHER, YOU'D PROBABLY MISS!

It was a cold, wet, miserable day and the goalie had had a bad match, allowing several goals through. As he sat moping in the dressing room, he sniffed and muttered, **'I think I've caught a cold.'**

'Thank goodness you can catch something,' said the captain.

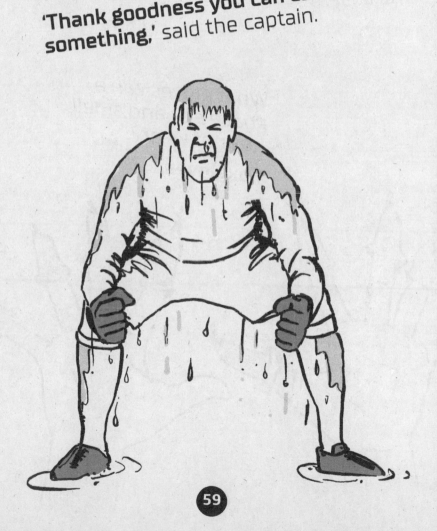

Manager: *Why are you late for training?*

Player: *I sprained my ankle.*

Manager: *That's a lame excuse.*

What gloves can a goalie see and smell but not wear?

Foxgloves.

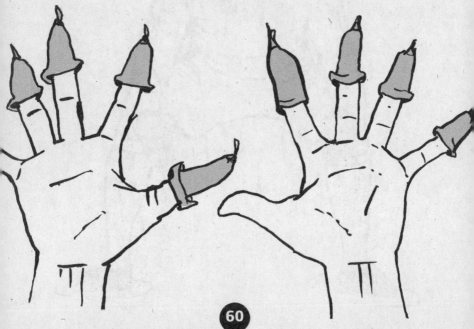

Player: *No one ever passes me the ball, I might as well be invisible.*

Manager: *Who said that?*

Renowned goalkeeper Jim 'Big Hands' O'Reilly was walking down the street.

'**I recognize him,**' said the man. '**But what's his name?**'

'**That's Big Hands,**' replied his friend.

'**Oh, really?**'

'**No, O'Reilly.**'

What wears out football boots but has no feet?

The ground.

What's the difference between an oak tree and a tight football boot?

One makes acorns, the other makes corns ache.

What do jelly babies wear on their feet when they play football?

Gumboots.

What did the football sock say to the football boot?

Well, I'll be darned!

Have you seen the new film about referees?

It's called the Umpire Strikes Back.

Who hangs out the washing on a football pitch?

The linesman.

Why did the referee have a sausage stuck behind his ear?

Because he'd eaten his whistle at lunchtime.

Did you hear about the footballer who ate little bits of metal all day?

It was his staple diet.

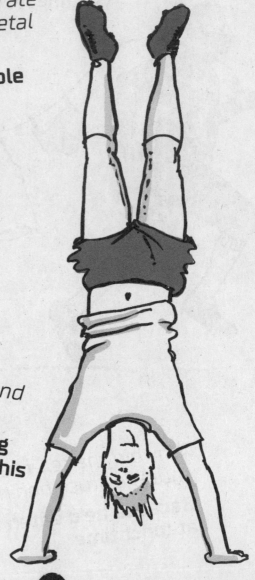

Why did the footballer stand on his head?

He was turning things over in his mind.

When is a football coach
not a football coach?

**After it's dropped the
players off.**

I've driven a football
coach for thirty years
and never had an
accident.

**I guess that makes me
a wreck-less driver.**

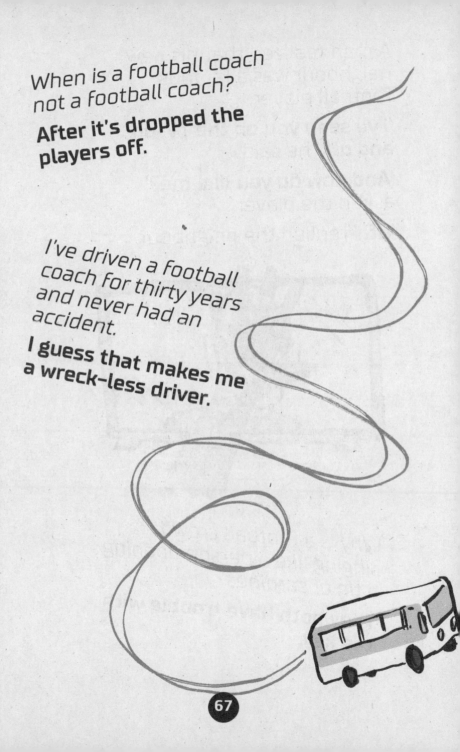

A man realized that his new neighbour was a famous football player.

'I've seen you on the TV, on and off,' he said.

'And how do you like me?' asked the player.

'Off,' replied the neighbour.

Why is a football crowd singing like a person opening a tin of sardines?

They both have trouble with the key.

Why is a referee like a kettle?

They both whistle when they're hot.

Which part of a football coach is the laziest?

The wheels, they're always tyred.

Football Practise

Teacher: What form are you in?

Student: Well, I scored two goals last Saturday.

The new boy came off the pitch looking miserable and slunk into the dressing room.

'**I've never played so badly before,**' he sighed.

'**Oh,**' answered his classmate. '**You've played before have you?**'

Teacher: And why were you late for school today?

Pupil: I was dreaming about a football match and they went into extra time.

Teacher: Who can explain to me what net profit is?

Pupil: When your team wins 6-0.

Father: Why are you taking the baby's bib out with you? I thought you were going to football practise?

Son: I am, but the coach said we'd be dribbling this week.

A man was frying some eggs for breakfast. Suddenly his daughter burst into the kitchen.

'**Careful! Careful!**' she yelled. '**Put in some more butter! Oh nuts! You're cooking too many at once. TOO MANY! Turn them! TURN THEM NOW! We need more butter. Oh no! Where are we going to get more BUTTER? They're going to STICK! Careful! CAREFUL! I said CAREFUL! You NEVER listen to me when you're cooking! Never! Turn them! Hurry up! Are you crazy? Have you lost your mind? Don't forget to salt them. You know you always forget to salt them. Use the salt! USE THE SALT! THE SALT!**'

Her father stared at her. '**What's wrong with you? You think I don't know how to fry a couple of eggs?**'

The daughter calmly replied, '**I just wanted to show you what it feels like when I'm trying to play football.**'

At one point during a football match, the coach called one of his twelve-year-old players aside and asked, '**Do you understand what cooperation is? What a team is?**'

The boy nodded. '**Do you understand that what matters is whether we win or lose together as a team?**'

The boy nodded again. '**So,**' the coach continued, '**I'm sure you know that when a corner is given, you shouldn't argue, swear or call the ref rude names. Do you understand all that?**'

Again the boy nodded. He continued, '**And when I take you off so another boy gets a chance to play, it's not good sportsmanship to call your coach a "useless pudding", is it?**'

Looking slightly ashamed by now, the boy agreed. '**Good,**' said the coach. '**Now go over there and explain all that to your mum.**'

Girl: Mum, can I go out and play?

Mum: What, with those holes in your socks?

Girl: No, with Billy next door – he's got a new football!'

The new manager of our struggling football team is strict and won't stand any nonsense.

Last Saturday, he spotted two fans climbing over the stadium wall and was absolutely livid. He grabbed them and yelled: **'Get back in there and watch the game until it finishes!'**

A scout was talking to a young player who had applied for a try-out with the club.

'**Can you kick with both feet?**' asked the scout.

'**Don't be silly!**' said the player. '**If I did that, I'd fall flat on my bum!**'

'Dad, I think I might have been picked for a position in the school team!'

'Really? That's great! But why do you only *think* you've been picked? And what position?'

'Well, the team hasn't been announced yet. But I overheard the coach talking to my teacher, and he said that if I was in the team I'd be a great drawback.'

You've got your boots on the wrong feet.

I can't have – these are the only feet I've got.

PRIVATE

Two boys were trespassing on the local football pitch and the groundsman came out and shouted at them.

'Didn't you see that sign?' he yelled.

'Yes, but it said "Private" at the top so we didn't think we should read any further,' replied the boys.

Knock, Knock on the Dressing Room Door

Knock, knock.

Who's there?

Waiter.

Waiter who?

Waiter minute while I tie my bootlaces.

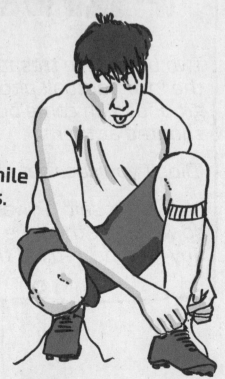

Knock, knock.

Who's there?

Farmer.

Farmer who?

Farmer birthday I got a new pair of football boots.

Knock, knock.

Who's there?

Omar.

Omar who?

Omar goodness, what a shot!

Knock, knock.

Who's there?

Gladys.

Gladys who?

Gladys Saturday – we can go to the match.

Knock, knock.

Who's there?

Philippa.

Philippa who?

Philippa bath – I'm covered in mud.

Knock, knock.

Who's there?

Stan.

Stan who?

Stan back – I'm going to shoot.

Knock, knock.

Who's there?

Fred.

Fred who?

Fred I can't play today, I've got a cold.

Knock, knock.

Who's there?

Norma Lee.

Norma Lee who?

Norma Lee I play in goal but today I'm at left back.

Knock, knock.

Who's there?

Police.

Police who?

Police let me play with your new football.

Knock, knock.

Who's there?

Justin.

Justin who?

Justin time to see us lose!

Knock, knock.

Who's there?

Anna.

Anna who?

Anna rack keeps you warm after football.

Knock, knock.

Who's there?

Saul.

Saul who?

Saul over when the final whistle blows.

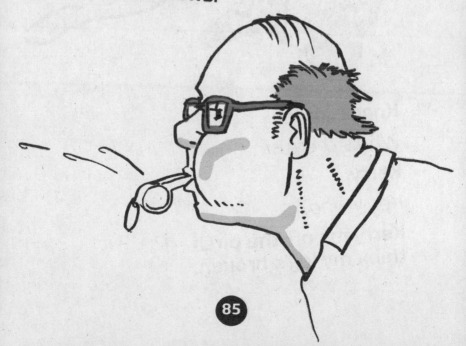

Knock, knock.

Who's there?

Aladdin.

Aladdin who?

Aladdin the street's waiting for you to come out and play football.

Knock, knock.

Who's there?

Kerry.

Kerry who?

Kerry me off the pitch – I think my leg's broken.

Knock, knock.

Who's there?

Mister.

Mister who?

Mister bus, that's why I'm late for the match.

Knock, knock.

Who's there?

Albie.

Albie who?

Albie home straight after the match.

Knock, knock.
Who's there?
Althea.
Althea who?
Althea later, down at the club.

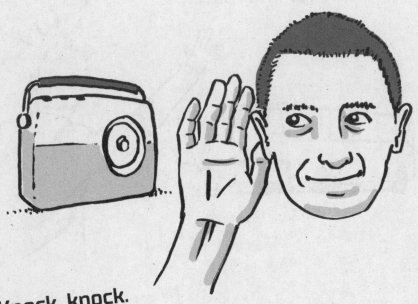

Knock, knock.
Who's there?
Alison.
Alison who?
Alison to the football results on the radio.

Knock, knock.
Who's there?
Euripides.
Euripides who?
Euripedes shorts and I won't buy you another pair.

Knock, knock.
Who's there?
Buster.
Buster who?
Buster Old Trafford, please.

Knock, knock.
Who's there?
Juno.
Juno who?
Juno what time kick-off is?

Knock, knock.
Who's there?
Howell.
Howell who?
Howell you take that corner?

Knock, knock.

Who's there?

Weed.

Weed who?

Weed like to win this game.

Knock, knock.

Who's there?

Godfrey.

Godfrey who?

Godfrey tickets for the match on Saturday.

Knock, knock.

Who's there?

Oily.

Oily who?

Oily in the morning's the best time to train.

Knock, knock.

Who's there?

Ammonia.

Ammonia who?

Ammonia little boy and I can't run as fast as you.

Knock, knock.
Who's there?
Macho.
Macho who?
Macho the Day.

Knock, knock.
Who's there?
General Lee.
General Lee who?
**General Lee I support Chelsea
but today I'm rooting for Fulham.**

Knock, knock.

Who's there?

Ida.

Ida who?

Ida terrible time getting to the match – all the buses were full!

Knock, knock.

Who's there?

Ammon.

Ammon who?

Ammon awfully good football player. Can I be in your team?

Knock, knock.
Who's there?
Stu.
Stu who?
Stu late to score a goal now!

Knock, knock.
Who's there?
Luke.
Luke who?
Luke, they've just scored a goal!

Clubs and Players

Olivier Giroud was stretchered off in a lot of pain and taken straight to the doctor. **'It's bad, Doc,'** he said through gritted teeth. **'When I touch my knee, it hurts. When I touch my stomach, it hurts. When I touch my elbow, it hurts. Everywhere I touch, it hurts!'**

'I've worked out the problem,' said the doctor. **'You've broken your finger.'**

How many Wigan fans
does it take to change
a light bulb?

Both of them.

What has legs like John Terry, a
face like John Terry and arms like
John Terry, yet isn't John Terry?

A photograph of John Terry.

What do Lionel Messi and a magician have in common?

Both do hat tricks.

How does Ronaldo change a light bulb?

He holds it in the air and the world revolves around him.

John Terry was talking through the park with a pig on a lead.

'That's unusual, where did you get him?' asked a passer-by.

'I won him in a raffle,' said the pig.

Which former Manchester United player never scored a goal?

George Worst.

Which football team never meets before a match?

Queen's Park Strangers.

After moving to Man. City, Raheem Sterling celebrated by buying some really fast chocolates.

Ferrari Rocher.

To celebrate a goal, Romelu Lukaku likes to lie down on the grass and rotate his body to propel himself sideways.

But that's just the way he rolls.

How many Man. United fans does it take to change a light bulb?

Three – the first to change the light bulb, the second to buy the commemorative Manchester United Light Bulb Change DVD and the third to drive the other two back to London.

Who is a horse's favourite player?

Neigh-mar.

Old Tony had been retired from the game for many years, but he still liked to tell people how good he'd once been.

'**They still remember me, you know,**' he said. '**Only yesterday, when I was at Old Trafford, there were lots of press photographers queuing to take my picture.**'

'**Really?**' said a disbelieving listener.

'**Yes. And if you don't believe me, ask David Beckham – he was standing next to me.**'

Which football team should you not eat in a sandwich?

Oldham.

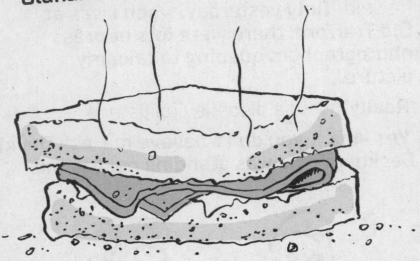

Someone has broken into Newcastle United's trophy room and stripped it clean.

Police have asked people to look out for anyone trying to sell six dusty shelves and a black-and-white carpet.

Which team keeps its boots in the fridge?

Tottenham Coldspur.

What blows at 100mph and always scores?

A Harrykane.

What's the difference between Aston Villa and a vase of flowers?

You can imagine a vase of flowers on top of a table.

THE SWEETEST STARS

Sergio Agu-**AERO**

Lee **KIT-KAT**-termole

MARS Bender

ROLO Toure

John **TERRY'S CHOCOLATE ORANGE**

WHO'S GOOD ENOUGH TO EAT?

Bacary **LASAGNE**

HAM SALAD–yce

Francis **COQ AU VIN**

PIZZA Crouch

Andy **CARROT**

Lionel **ETON MESS**–i

CHOCOLATE MOUSSE–a
Dembele

Alan **MUTTON**

In 2006 the architect was showing the Arsenal team around the new Emirates stadium. **'I think you'll find it's completely flawless,'** he said proudly.

'What do we walk on, then?' asked Theo Walcott.

Which football team travels around in an ice-cream truck?

Aston Vanilla.

Bolton have got a tough game this weekend.

They've got to play football.

Which team spends its spare time in nightclubs?

Blackburn Ravers.

Manchester United were playing Chelsea at Stamford Bridge. A man wearing a bright red and white rosette walked up to the ticket office and asked the price of admission.

'**Twenty pounds, sir,**' said the attendant.

'**Here's ten pounds,**' replied the man. '**There's only one team worth watching.**'

What is Wayne Rooney's favourite meal?

Fish and chipping.

Michael Owen is going to release a perfume next year.

He's calling it 'My Cologne'.

Which footballer
makes a lot of
coffee?
Diego Costa.

Which player do
sheep like best?
Paul PogBAA.

Which footballer keeps the house warm in winter?

Ashley Cole.

Why is Ronaldo's bedroom always tidy?

Because he's not Messi!

Extra Time

Why did the two footballers get married?

Because they were the perfect match.

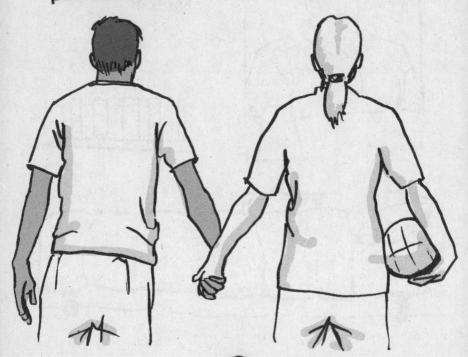

If you have a referee in football and an umpire in cricket, what do you have in bowls?

Goldfish.

What do you call a referee wearing five balaclavas on a cold day?

Anything you like – he can't hear you.

A tourist visiting London stopped a man carrying a football and asked, '**How do I get to Wembley?**'

'**Practise**', the man replied.

Footballer: I've had an idea that might help us win a few matches.

Captain: Good. When are you leaving?

What did the pitch say to the player?

I hate it when people treat me like dirt.

When is a kick like a boat?

When it's a punt.

What did the ball say to
the footballer?

I get a kick out of you.

What's yellow, has
twenty-two legs and
peels off at half time?

Banana United.

What's black and white and wears dark glasses?

A football in disguise.

What two things should a footballer never eat before breakfast?

Lunch and dinner.

If it takes twenty men six months to build a grandstand at the football pitch, how long would it take forty men to build it?

No time at all, because the twenty men have already completed it!

A lad had a great seat in the front row. His neighbour asked how he got his ticket.

'I got it from my brother,' he replied. **'He can't come.'**

'Why not?'

'He's stuck at home . . . looking for his ticket.'

Which member
of the team flies
down the field?

The winger.

Why did the fans set fire
to the stadium?

**Because they had a burning
interest in football.**

Player 1: Why do you call the manager 'Camera'?
Player 2: Because he's always snapping at me.

Despite the fact that the new player was trying his best, he was very disappointing.

You see, you don't need tries in football!

Scottish captain: *How can we raise the level of our game?*

Scottish manager: *Let's play at the top of Ben Nevis.*

Manager: *'This dressing room is disgusting! It hasn't been cleaned for a month!'*

Cleaner: *'Don't blame me, I've only been here for a fortnight.'*

Why was the footballer upset on her birthday?

She got a red card.

What do you call a referee with three eyes?

Seymour.

Why did the boy swallow a plum whole?

His doctor told him that if he wanted to play football, he'd have to gain at least a stone.

What's a goalkeeper's favourite snack?

Beans on post.

When does a football pitch turn into a triangle?

When a player takes a corner.

My old computer's caught that 'Bad-Goalie' virus...

Now it can't save anything.

Which player brings a rope on to the pitch?

The skipper.

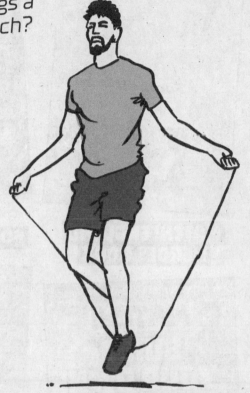

What's the best position to play if you don't like football?

Right back – right back in the dressing room.

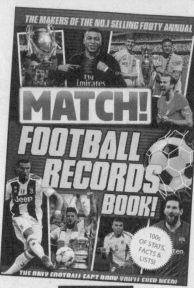